Collins

Knowledge Lighthouse 3

A skill-based course on General Knowledge

Seema Chari
Kunal Savarkar

Student + Teacher			Teacher-only	
a animations	**ia** activities	**g** games	**lp** lesson plans	**tn** teacher's notes
ilt instructor-led tutorials	**w** worksheets	**v** videos	**w** worksheets	**ak** answer keys
	audio			

Preface

There is no single route to knowledge and its sources are as diverse as the paths we adopt to gather and retain it, right from our family, school and friends to the Internet and books. General Knowledge is like common sense, but in times of multimedia, while it is easily available and accessible, it is not always easy to distinguish between real and fake, relevant and redundant, and interesting and inconsequential. We live in the digital age, which requires constant flexibility and adaptability.

Knowledge Lighthouse is a series meant for the Gen Z, or learners born in the new millennium. Their professional requirements are drastically different from those of earlier generations and require 'upskilling' throughout their lives. The series covers the general knowledge quotient of a spectrum of curricular as well as extra-curricular domains for learners of grades 1 to 8, with special emphasis on 21st century skills. They are divided into three segments—learning skills, literacy skills and life skills. Through this series, we are certain that all learners can attain knowledge as the tasks are 'workoutable' and grade-appropriate.

General Knowledge provides context to school curriculum. *Knowledge Lighthouse* books are a repository of varied tasks divided in eight themes and skill pages. Our country is often presented in a complicated or insufficient way in GK books. This series showcases India content through colourful, simple and exciting tasks. Within the vast and varied India chapters are brand-new features such as state-focus, city-focus and visit-a-monument.

Science, technology, engineering and mathematics (STEM), the disciplines of the future that add a sprinkle of trivia to otherwise serious subjects have been covered extensively in grades 6-8.

The protection of our planet and sustainable development are critical issues that all of us need to think about and be aware of. Save the Planet theme aims to sensitise learners towards sustainable development throughout the series.

In the Skills pages, life skills has tasks on safety and self-awareness. Connecting the dots is the foundation of knowledge and the series has chapters based on Higher Order Thinking Skills (HOTS) and critical thinking to train young minds to see patterns, learn to eliminate or choose details and observe better.

Become a Champion Quizzer

Knowledge Lighthouse encourages all learners to be curious and explore the world around them. Those who observe and absorb all the time, learn from everyone and everything; they are the ones who become quizzers! Here are six rules that will help you become a champion quizzer.

1. Be curious—look around you, see everything, read everything.
2. Listen to others.
3. Seek out new experiences.
4. Learn to link events and people.
5. Do your own research and learn to spot fake news.
6. Remember, no matter how much you know, there is much more that you have yet to learn.

Now, go for it! We are sure that this series will expose a whole new generation of learners to the fun universe of general knowledge, and enhance their love for learning and discovery.

~ Kunal Savarkar and Seema Chari

In this series ...

Knowledge Lighthouse tasks are thematic and linear with visual, verbal, and strategic inputs to help students solve them and acquire knowledge through a wide range of subjects and themes.

World Around Us tasks take the learners on an exciting journey across the world.

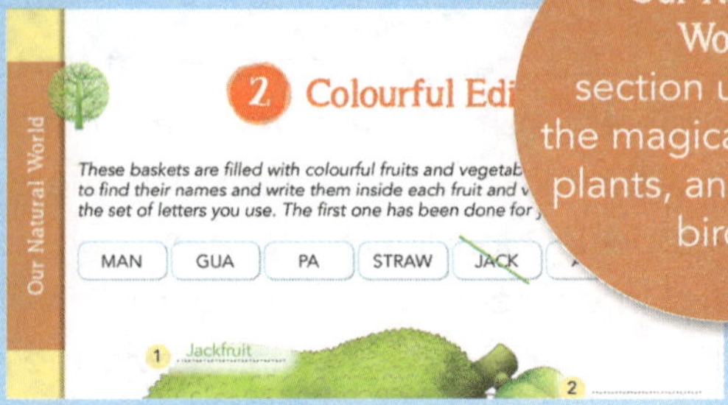

Our Natural World section uncovers the magical realm of plants, animals and birds.

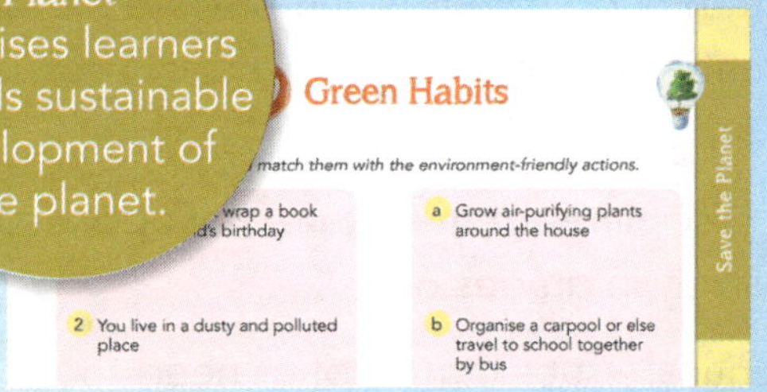

Save the Planet sensitises learners towards sustainable development of the planet.

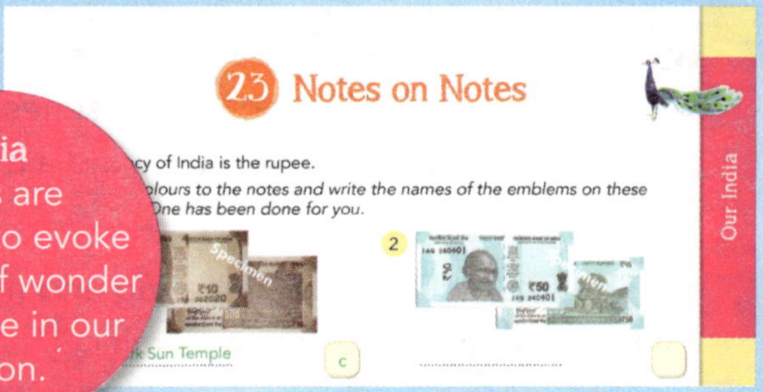

India tasks are created to evoke a sense of wonder and pride in our nation.

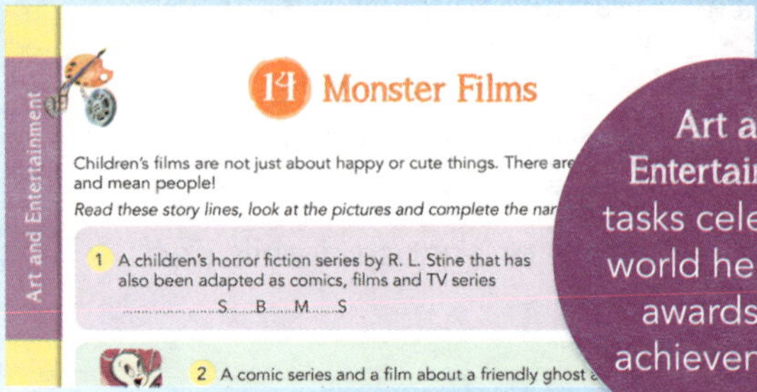

Art and Entertainment tasks celebrates world heritage, awards and achievements.

Sports and Games section provides rules and records related to different sports.

Language and Literature tasks present vocabulary and etymology in a fun way.

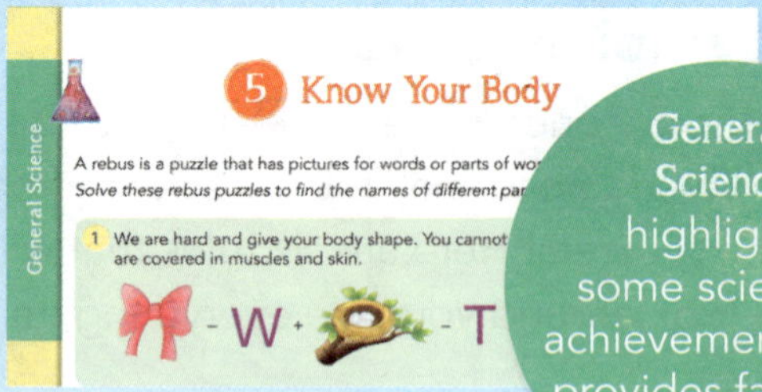

General Science highlights some scientific achievements and provides facts for others.

Whiz Fact is a spin-off fact about each topic or theme.

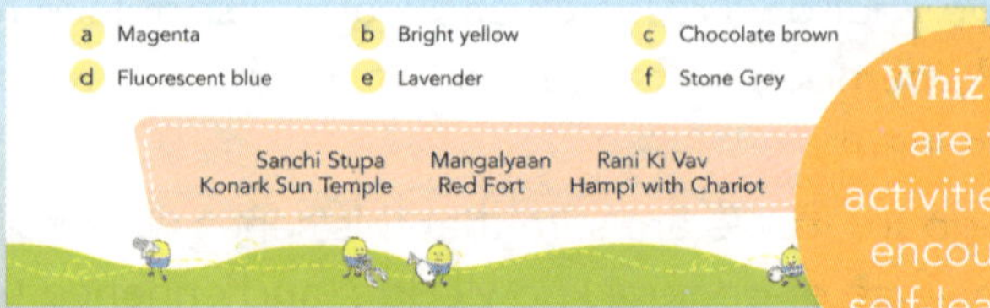

Whiz Quiz are fun activities that encourage self-learning.

21st Century Skills

21st century skills are necessary to succeed in the Age of Information. These skills are divided into three main sets, namely, learning skills, literacy skills and life skills.

Learning Skills

- Critical Thinking and HOTS
- Creativity
- Collaboration
- Communication

Literacy Skills

- Technology
- Information
- Media

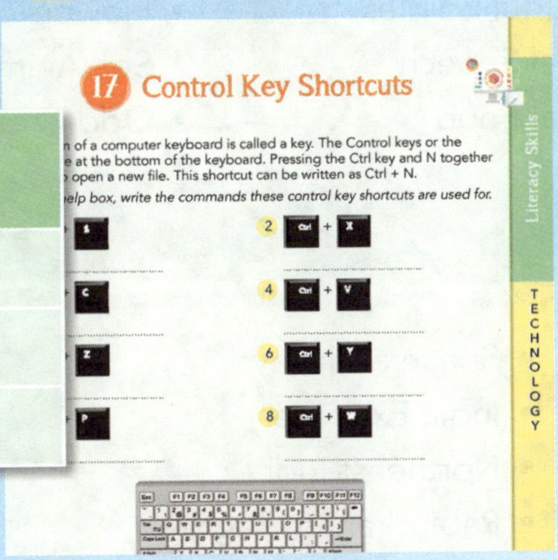

Life Skills

- Problem-solving
- Self-awareness
- Safety
- Social Skills

Detailed Contents

General Science

- Know Your Body
- Famous Inventions

Sports and Games

- Indoor Games
- Ball Games
- Sports Champions
- Athletic Fun
- Olympics Special

Save the Planet

- Green Habits

Learning Skills

- Things Take Time
- Picture Puzzles
- Celestial Objects
- Anagrams
- Sudoku

Literacy Skills

- Control Key Shortcuts
- Fun with Wrappers
- Closed Lists

Life Skills

- Being Safe
- Mind and Body
- Camping Time

Contents

1 What is the Good Word?

Some words sound the same but are spelled differently.

Fill in the blanks using the words given in the help box.

1 

We took turns, ... at a time.

2 

Miriam was going for a walk, the cat wanted to come ....

3 

The bird is singing over ....

4 

The children are helping .... mother.

5 

.... a good day to stay home and read.

6 

The dog kept wagging .... tail.

it's their too there its two

Whiz Fact

Sometimes two words can be joined to form shorter words. For example, 'what is' can be written as what's and 'you are' can be written as you're. A symbol called an apostrophe (') is used to indicate that one or more letters have been left out of a word.

Our Natural World

2 Colourful Edibles

These baskets are filled with colourful fruits and vegetables. Join the letters to find their names and write them inside each fruit and vegetable. Strike out the set of letters you use. The first one has been done for you.

MAN	GUA	PA	STRAW	~~JACK~~	APRI	CHER

~~FRUIT~~	PAYA	GO	VA	RY	COT	BERRY

Whiz Fact

Tomatoes are actually fruits of plants. They are the main ingredient of red pizza and pasta sauces.

CAP	CAB	CAULI	PUMP	PO	SPI

NACH	SICUM	TATO	FLOWER	BAGE	KIN

Whiz Quiz

1. Name a fruit which is eaten raw in salads.

   ....

2. Name a fruit that can be cooked.

   ....

3 Mice Rhymes

One is a mouse, the plural is mice. Read this rhyme about a mouse.

Hickory dickory dock.
The mouse ran up the clock.
The clock struck one,
The mouse ran down,
Hickory dickory dock.

Let us write an acrostic poem. Each line should begin with the letters of the word 'mouse'. Here is an example.

M	y house
O	n the hill
U	sed to be
S	o full of mice
E	ek!

Now write acrostic poems using letters of the words 'tiger' and 'horse'.

1

T ....

I ....

G ....

E ....

R ....

2

H ....

O ....

R ....

S ....

E ....

Whiz Fact

Walt Disney wanted to create a cartoon animal in place of a rabbit named Oswald. His new animal was none other than Mickey Mouse!

4 Animal Speech

Animals cannot talk. The sounds they make help other animals, and sometimes even human beings understand what they might be trying to say. Many common words are also used to describe the sounds that animals make.

Fill in the blanks using the words given in the help box. Use the same word to fill both blanks in each question.

1 When it is cold, our teeth ....

Monkeys ....

2 We select with the .... of a mouse.

Dolphins ....

3 A .... is a musical instrument which produces a loud sound.

Elephants ....

4 A .... is a black bird.

Roosters ....

Parrots and parakeets are talking birds. They can mimic the speech of human beings.

5 When stuck in a traffic jam, drivers often ....

Geese ....

6 The outside of a tree trunk is called a ....

Dogs ....

7 When someone cracks a joke, we ....

Hyenas ....

8 When a nice song plays, we .... along.

Whales ....

9 When door hinges are not oiled, they ....

Mice ....

10 When we try to sing with a sore throat, we ....

Frogs ....

trumpet	click	bark	chatter	honk
sing	crow	laugh	squeak	croak

Whiz Quiz

Name the animals that make these sounds.

1 Bray ....

2 Purr ....

5 Know Your Body

A rebus is a puzzle that has pictures for words or parts of words.

Solve these rebus puzzles to find the names of different parts of the body.

1 We are hard and give your body shape. You cannot see us because we are covered in muscles and skin.

 – W +  – T = ...

2 I am a bit larger than your fist. I pump blood through your body.

 – N + 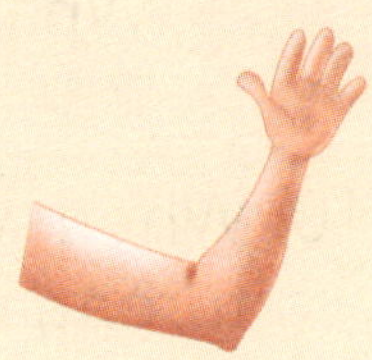 – M + T = ...

3 I am inside your head and look like a shelled walnut. I help you to think and learn.

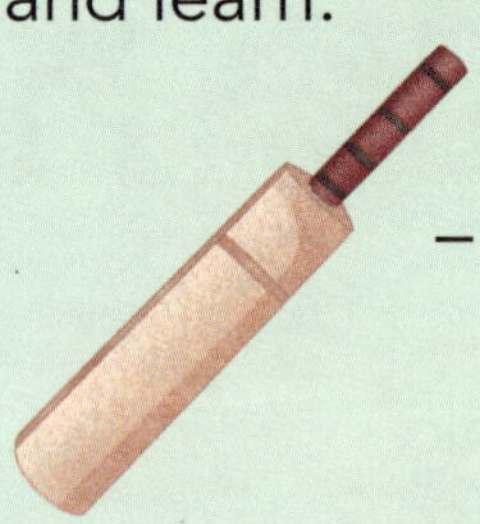 – A T +  = ...

Whiz Fact

The bony case in which our brain and sense organs are enclosed is called the skull. It is made up of 22 bones which are joined.

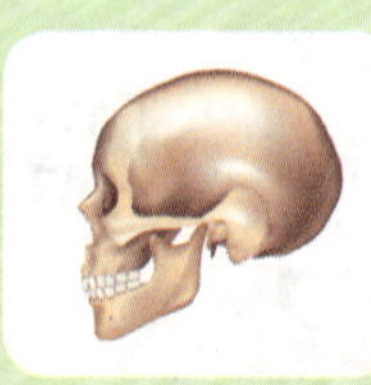

4 I am the largest organ in the body and I am very thin.

 - Y +  - DIA = ...

5 I am curved and help you stand straight.

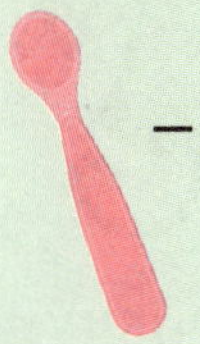 - OON + 9 - N = ...

6 Once you swallow food, it reaches me. I help you digest the food and give you energy.

 - OL + 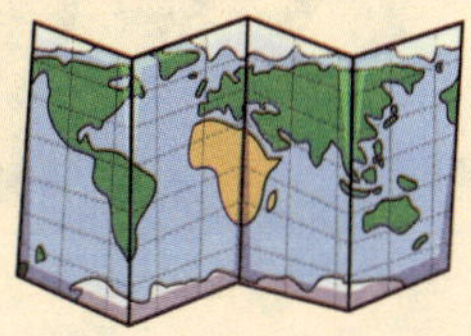 - P +  - AIR

= ....

7 We are a pair and help you to breathe. The air you take in reaches us.

 - CH +  - OAT + S

= ....

Whiz Quiz Which is the only bone of the skull that can move?

6 Animal Food

Look at the pictures of these animals and write H for herbivores, C for carnivores and O for omnivores.

1 
Horse

2 
Rat

3 
Fox

4 
Monkey

5 
Cow

6 
Donkey

7 
Bear

8 
Dog

9 
Lion

10 
Camel

11 
Tiger

Whiz Fact

The giant panda, which belongs to the bear family, feeds only on bamboo.

7 Indoor Games

Look at the pictures and write the names of these indoor games using the words given in the help box.

1 

....

2 

....

3 

....

4 

....

5 

....

6 

....

7 

....

8 

....

9 

....

Jenga Scrabble Monopoly Snakes and Ladders
Ludo Carrom Lego Battleship Chess

8 Flowers Galore

Flowers are used for more than just decoration.

Read the clues and look at the pictures. Write the names of these flowers using words from the help box.

1 A fragrant flower called *champa* in Hindi. It is used for making incense.

....

2 This flower is also known as moringa. We eat a long stick-like vegetable that grows on its plant.

....

3 A flower which grows on a huge tree that gives us shade.

....

4 A beautiful flower poets write about. It closes in the night and grows mostly in mountainous regions.

....

5 Small roundish flowers that grow in bunches. They are pink, violet and even dark blue.

....

6 A flower used as a spice. It is also gives us oil.

....

7 This flower can be pink, purple or even white. It grows in huge bushes. We often see it growing on walls.

....

8 A red or white flower used as tea. It is also used for decoration.

....

pansy	frangipani	bougainvillea	drumstick flower
daffodil	hibiscus	gulmohar flower	clove flower

Whiz Fact

Flowers such as sunflowers and daisies are composite flowers. They are made up of many tiny flowers that appear like a single flower.

9 My Favourite Books

Write the names of the books with the help of the clues. Take one word from each help box and join them to find the names some popular children's books.

1 Mowgli is brought up by a wolf pack.

The ....

2 A girl falls into a rabbit hole.

.... Adventures in ....

3 A man travels to the land of tiny people.

....

4 A mouse is adopted by a family.

....

5 A bear whose best friend is a piglet.

.... -the- ....

Alice's Charlotte's Black Gulliver's Winnie
Pippi Bear Stuart Jungle Peter

6 A spider is the heroine of this book.

....

7 This little boy could fly but never grew up.

....

8 A nine-year-old girl lives with her pet monkey and pet horse in a little Swedish village.

....

9 A bear from Darkest Peru moves in with a family in London.

A .... Called ....

10 A horse tells the story of its life.

....

Pan	Travels	Web	Little	Paddington
Longstockings	Beauty	Book	Pooh	Wonderland

Whiz Fact

A Little Pretty Pocket-Book written by John Newbery is considered the first modern children's book. It is a mix of rhymes, picture stories and games.

10 Respected Indians

These Indians are respected for their achievements. Fill in the blanks using the words given in the help box. Each question has two answers.

1 The former ………………………… of India, he is known as the Missile Man of India. He was a ………………………… before he became the President.

A. P. J. Abdul Kalam

Mother Teresa

2 An Albanian nun, she came to ………………………… and set up homes and clinics for the poor. She received the ………………………… in 1979 and was named a saint after her death.

3 She was a classical dancer who set up an academy for arts called …………………………. She learnt ………………………… from the famous Russian dancer, Anna Pavlova.

Rukmini Devi Arundale

4 One of the greatest .... players of India, he won three Olympic .... medals. His birthday is celebrated as the National Sports Day in India.

Dhyan Chand

Sarojini Naidu

5 Also known as the .... of India, she was a famous freedom fighter and a .... She was born in present-day Telangana.

6 He was the first .... of India. His birthday is celebrated as ....

Jawaharlal Nehru

Kalakshetra	scientist	Prime Minister	Nobel Peace Prize	
ballet	Children's Day	President	Kolkata	lawyer
gold	nightingale	hockey	poet	

Whiz Fact

Sardar Vallabhbhai Patel is known as the Iron Man of India. He is regarded as one of the most important leaders of India's freedom struggle.

11 Sea Animals

Fill in the blanks with the names of some sea animals given in the help box.

1 An .... has eight limbs.

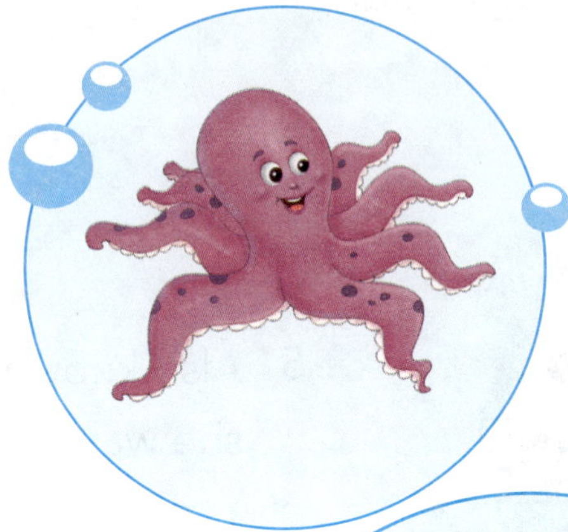

2 A .... has a water spout on its head.

3 A .... has five arms and looks like a star.

4 A .... has a head and many long wavy tentacles.

Whiz Fact

Creatures living in the sea breathe through gills. Whales and dolphins come to the surface of water to breathe and then go back in the water.

5 A .... is tiny. Its head looks like a horse's head and it has a curvy curled-up tail.

6 A .... is a very big fish with many sharp, curved teeth.

7 An .... has two shells. Sometimes it makes pearls.

8 A .... has two huge claws and many pointy legs.

shark	octopus	oyster	seahorse
whale	crab	jellyfish	starfish

12 Ball Games

Find names of 10 common ball games in the word search and then write their names.

B	F	Z	N	Y	T	C	W	X	U	K	D	W
O	B	A	S	K	E	T	B	A	L	L	N	G
W	G	N	Q	W	N	V	I	Q	N	I	E	X
L	H	O	U	A	N	O	L	I	N	G	O	R
I	U	R	A	T	I	A	L	H	U	L	A	V
N	K	K	S	E	S	F	I	O	A	Y	M	O
G	W	E	H	M	G	C	A	C	Z	E	R	L
G	T	L	L	S	O	U	R	K	B	Y	R	L
O	B	L	N	K	W	Y	D	E	I	Y	U	E
L	Q	I	L	A	C	K	S	Y	O	S	G	Y
F	I	N	W	I	N	D	S	U	R	F	B	B
N	N	G	K	N	Y	M	P	H	E	T	Y	A
P	O	L	O	G	A	R	I	S	O	N	E	L

1 

....

2 

....

3 

....

4 

....

5

....

6

....

7

....

8

....

9

....

10

....

Whiz Quiz

Which of these is a popular bat-and-ball game of America?

a baseball b cricket c hockey

Whiz Fact

Lacrosse is a stick and ball game. The head of the stick has a net which is used to carry, pass or throw the ball into the goal. Lacrosse was first played in Canada.

13 Things Take Time

Read the starting time and the finishing time of the activities on the clocks and write how much time it took to do each activity.

1 Kunal started brushing his teeth at 7:24 a.m. and finished at 7:26 a.m.

.... hours .... minutes

2 The storm began at 12:35 p.m. and ended at 2:20 p.m.

.... hours .... minutes

3 The movie started at 11:45 a.m. and ended at 1:55 p.m.

.... hours .... minutes

4 The guests arrived at 5:50 p.m. and left at 9:00 p.m.

.... hours .... minutes

5 The bus started at 8:15 a.m. and arrived at the bus stop at 12:40 p.m.

.... hours .... minutes

6 The award ceremony began at 9:10 a.m. and ended at 10:30 a.m.

.... hours .... minutes

7 The hike began at 8:40 a.m. and ended at 10:05 a.m.

.... hours .... minutes

An hourglass or a sandglass can be used to measure time. It has two glass bulbs with a narrow 'neck' in between.

14 Monster Films

Children's films are not just about happy or cute things. They are about monsters and mean people too!

Read these story lines, look at the pictures and complete the names of the films.

1 A children's horror fiction series by R. L. Stine that has also been adapted as comics, films and TV series

....S........B........M........S

2 A comic series and a film about a friendly ghost and his three nasty ghost uncles

....SP........R

3 A movie about Dracula, his daughter, lots of monsters and one human

........OT........L ........RA........SYL........A........I........

4 A movie based on Roald Dahl's book, featuring Luke and his grandmother

....E ........IT........H........S

5 A movie about a wicked fairy who is also a fairy godmother, she places a curse on a young princess

........AL........FI........ ....NT

Whiz Fact

Count Dracula is a character based on a real person who lived in Romania. Thanks to Bram Stoker's novel by the same name, Dracula, the blood-sucking vampire became a huge and scary villain.

15 Camping Time

Tick (✓) the things you will need to pack for a 3-day camp.

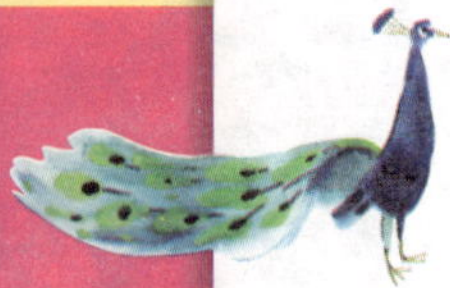

16 Taj Mahal

Complete the sentences about the Taj Mahal using the words given in the help box.

1. The Taj Mahal is a .... , which means a building that houses tombs.

2. It is located on the banks of the river .... in the city of Agra in Uttar Pradesh.

3. It was built using white .... from Makrana.

4. It has a huge onion-shaped ....

5. The Taj Mahal has four tall ....

6. It is surrounded by four lovely .... with water channels.

dome	minarets	Yamuna	mausoleum	marble	gardens

Whiz Fact

The Taj Mahal was built by the Mughal emperor Shah Jahan for his queen, Mumtaz Mahal.

17 Control Key Shortcuts

Each button of a computer keyboard is called a key. The Control keys or the Ctrl keys are at the bottom of the keyboard. Pressing the Ctrl key and N together allows us to open a new file. This shortcut can be written as Ctrl + N.

Using the help box, write the commands these control key shortcuts are used for.

1. Ctrl + S ....
2. Ctrl + X ....
3. Ctrl + C ....
4. Ctrl + V ....
5. Ctrl + Z ....
6. Ctrl + Y ....
7. Ctrl + P ....
8. Ctrl + W ....

Close file	Save file	Cut	Undo
Paste	Print	Copy	Redo

Whiz Fact

The shortcut Ctrl + A is used to select all text in a document.

18 Odd Creature Out

Circle the odd one in each row. With the help of the hints write why it is the odd one out.

1

a 
Penguin

b 
Kingfisher

c 
Sparrow

d 
Eagle

It is odd because ....

Hint: What do most birds do?

2

a 
Shark

b 
Cat

c 
Crocodile

d 
Frog

It is odd because ....

Hint: Where do these animals live?

3

a 
Snake

b 
Monkey

c 
Lizard

d 
Chameleon

It is odd because ....

Hint: What kind of skin do these animals have?

4 a 
Lion fish

b 
Dolphin

c 
Whale

d 
Goldfish

It is odd because ....

Hint: How do these animals breathe?

5 a 
Ant

b 
Bee

c 
Cockroach

d 
Spider

It is odd because ....

Hint: How many legs do these creatures have?

6 a 
Lobster

b 
Crab

c 
Prawn

d 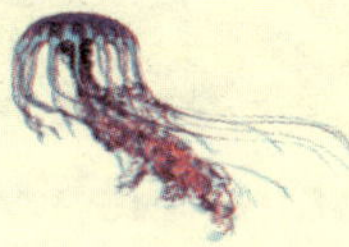
Jellyfish

It is odd because ....

Hint: What kind of body do these animals have?

Whiz Fact

Mammals are animals that give birth to their young ones. Monkeys, lions and human beings are mammals. Duck-billed platypus and spiny anteaters found in Australia, are mammals whose babies hatch from eggs.

19 Sports Champions

Look at the pictures and complete the names of the sports these sports champions play.

Leander Peas

1 ....NN.......... ....

Sania Mirza

Sakshi Malik

2 ....RE.......... ....LI..........G

Sushil Kumar

Saina Nehwal

3 ....MI.......... ....ON

P.V. Sindhu

Mithali Raj

4 ....IC.......... ....T

Bhuvneshwar Kumar

Whiz Fact

Five sportspersons were awarded the Rajiv Gandhi Khel Ratna in 2020. This is the highest number of awardees ever.

Abhinav Bindra

5 ....HO......... ....NG

Anjali Bhagwat

Vishwanathan Anand

6 ....ES.........

Koneru Humpy

Anirban Lahiri

7 ....L.........

Aditi Ashok

Mary Kom

8 ....ING

Vijender Singh

golf	tennis	badminton	wrestling
chess	boxing	shooting	cricket

Whiz Quiz Which sportspersons were awarded the Rajiv Gandhi Khel Ratna in August 2020?

20 Countries and Flags

Every country has a flag. Some flags look like one another. Colour these flags using the colour key.

(1) Red (2) White (3) Blue (4) Green

1 France

Russia

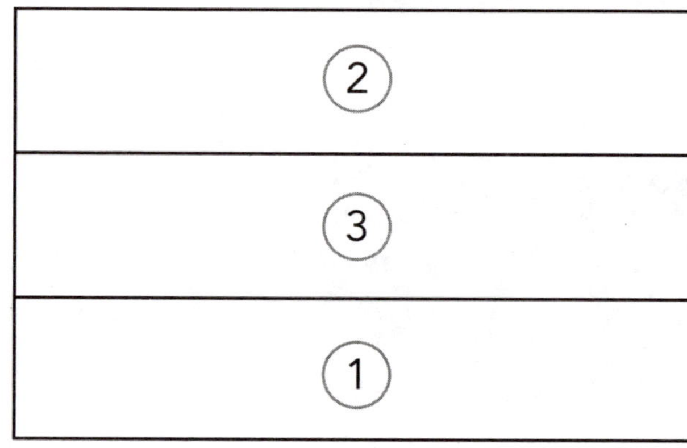

2 Italy

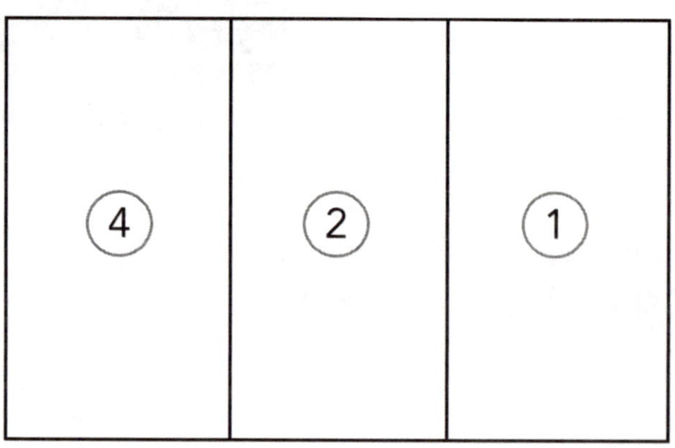

Hungary

3 Japan

Bangladesh

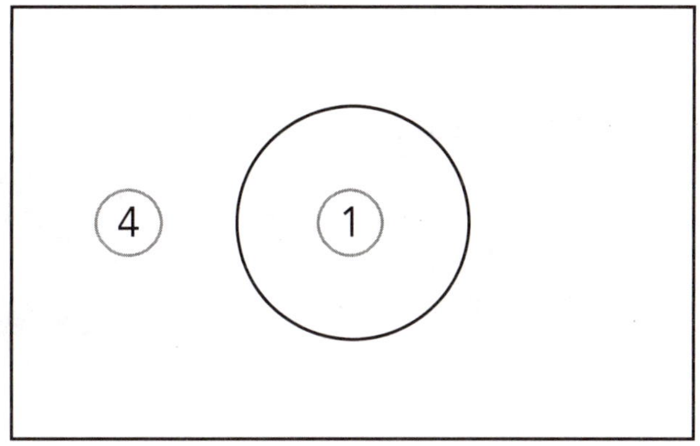

4 Turkey

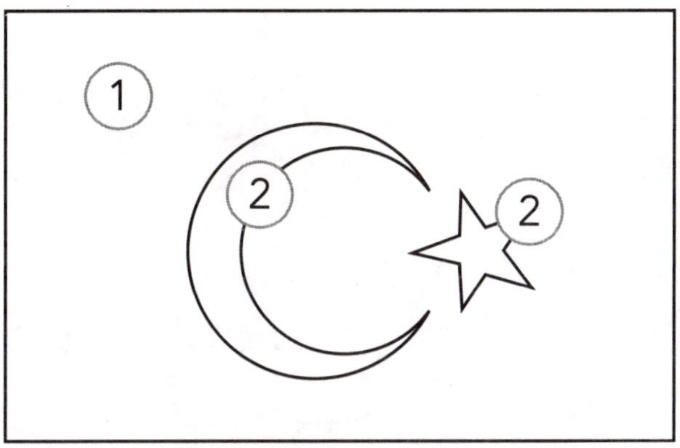

Pakistan

5 Poland

Indonesia

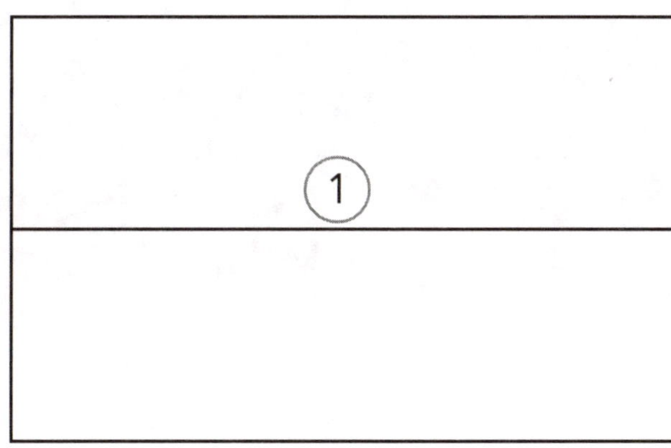

Whiz Fact

Most flags are rectangular but the flag of Nepal is the only one which looks like two triangles placed on top of one another.

21 Picture Puzzles

Label these pictures to solve these rebus puzzles. One has been done for you.

1  +  = 

Cup .... Cake .... Cupcake ....

2  - T +  = 

....

3 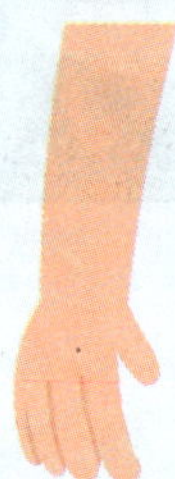 +  = 

....

4 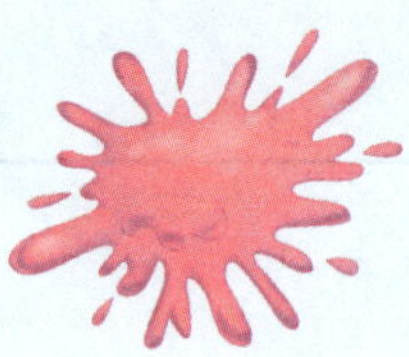 - P +  = 

....

5  + B +  = 

....

6  +  = 

....

7  - ET +  - G = 

....

8  + 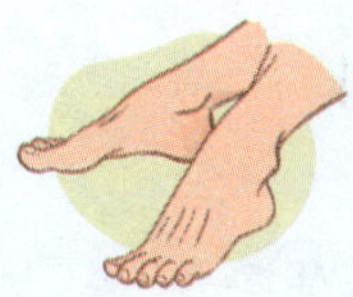 - FE = 

....

9  +  - T = 

....

10 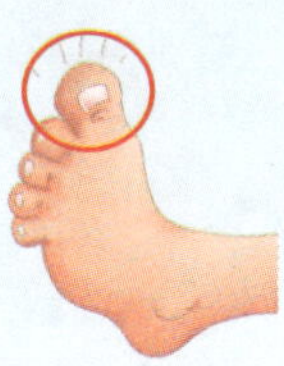 - E + A +  - AR = 

....

Whiz Fact

Rebuses can be quite complicated. Rebus M ce, M ce, M ce means 'Three Blind Mice'. This is because I's are missing from the words or 'no eyes'!

22 North, South, East, West

Have you seen a compass? The needle of a compass always points to the north. If we face north, the south is right behind us. The east is on our right and the west is on our left.

Look at the map of India. Some of the states and union territories have been coloured. Write whether these states are in the north, south, east, west or in the centre of India.

Whiz Fact

The largest state in India is Rajasthan and the smallest state is Goa.

23 Notes on Notes

The currency of India is the rupee.

Match the colours to the notes and write the names of the emblems on these bank notes. One has been done for you.

1

Konark Sun Temple c

2

.... ☐

3

.... ☐

4

.... ☐

5

.... ☐

6

.... ☐

Colours

- a Magenta
- b Bright yellow
- c Chocolate brown
- d Fluorescent blue
- e Lavender
- f Stone Grey

Sanchi Stupa | Mangalyaan | Rani Ki Vav | Konark Sun Temple | Red Fort | Hampi with Chariot

24 Interjections

Words that are used to express feelings such as joy, surprise or shock are called interjections. Sentences ending in interjections are followed by an exclamation mark (!).

Read the lines and choose the correct interjections from the help box and write them in the blanks provided.

1

A book fell right on your toe.

....

2

You show a beautiful drawing you made to your family.

....

3

You have just seen a huge crawly worm

....

4

Your mom had promised you a treat but she has just cancelled it.

....

Whiz Fact

Every language has its own interjections. In French and Italian, people yell *ayi-ayi-ayi-ayi*! when hurt.

5

Your parents just told you that they have booked tickets for a movie.

....

6

Your friend's father calls up to tell you that she has fallen sick.

....

7

Your friend has just done a headstand.

....

8

You are with your friend inside a church and he is talking noisily.

....

Yahoo!	Eek!	Wow!	Shh!
Boo-hoo!	Ouch!	Ta-da!	Oh no!

Whiz Quiz Find matching interjections in your language for the ones given in this chapter.

25 Celestial Objects

Using the letter code and the clues, find out the names of the planets of the solar system.

A =	©	M =	¶	S =	★	C =	§	N =	⌘	E =	∞
O =	ⓘ	U =	⏎	H =	◆	P =	⏏	J =	⊘	R =	≅
Y =	⌥	I =	^	T =	•	V =	≥				

1. The smallest planet named after a Roman God of the same name.

¶	∞	≅	§	⏎	≅	⌥

2. The planet known as the 'morning star' or the 'evening star'. The Sun rises in the west and sets in the east on this planet.

≥	∞	⌘	⏎	★

3. The only planet known to have life on it.

∞	©	≅	•	◆

Whiz Fact

Celestial objects that move around the planets are called satellites. The moon is the satellite of the Earth.

4 Also called the 'red planet', it is the neighbour of only planet that has life on it. India's space probe called Mangalyaan landed on its surface in 2014.

¶	©	≅	★

5 The largest planet in the solar system, it is named after the Roman sky god.

⊘	⏎	⏏	^	•	∞	≅

6 The planet with rings around it that can be seen at night without a telescope. A day of the week is named after it.

★	©	•	⏎	≅	⌘

7 Also known as the 'ice giant', it is not the farthest planet from the Sun and yet has the coldest temperature in the solar system.

⏎	≅	©	⌘	⏎	★

8 A planet blue in colour and named after the Roman god of the sea.

⌘	∞	⏏	•	⏎	⌘	∞

26 Famous Inventions

When something useful is made for the first time, it is called an invention. The person who makes an invention is called an inventor.

Read the clues and match the inventors to the inventions by writing letters in the boxes.

1

Orville Wright and Wilbur Wright

2

John Logie Baird

3

Thomas Alva Edison

4

Alexander Graham Bell

5

Antonio Meucci

6

Charles Babbage

Whiz Fact

The Chinese were great inventors. They invented paper, clocks and the compass.

a

Television

b

Aeroplane

c

Telephone

Clues

1. The Wright Brothers wondered how humans could fly.
2. John Logie Baird tried to find a way to watch programmes at home.
3. Thomas Alva Edison helped us have light even after sunset.
4. Alexander Graham Bell and Antonio Meucci found out how to make sound travel from one place to the other.
5. Charles Babbage invented a machine which allowed all kinds of calculations.

e

Bulb

d

Computer

Whiz Quiz

Who invented these instruments?

1. Telescope ....
2. Camera ....

27 Fun with Wrappers

Every food product we buy has some information on its wrapper. Let us try to understand some terms or markings used on food wrappers.

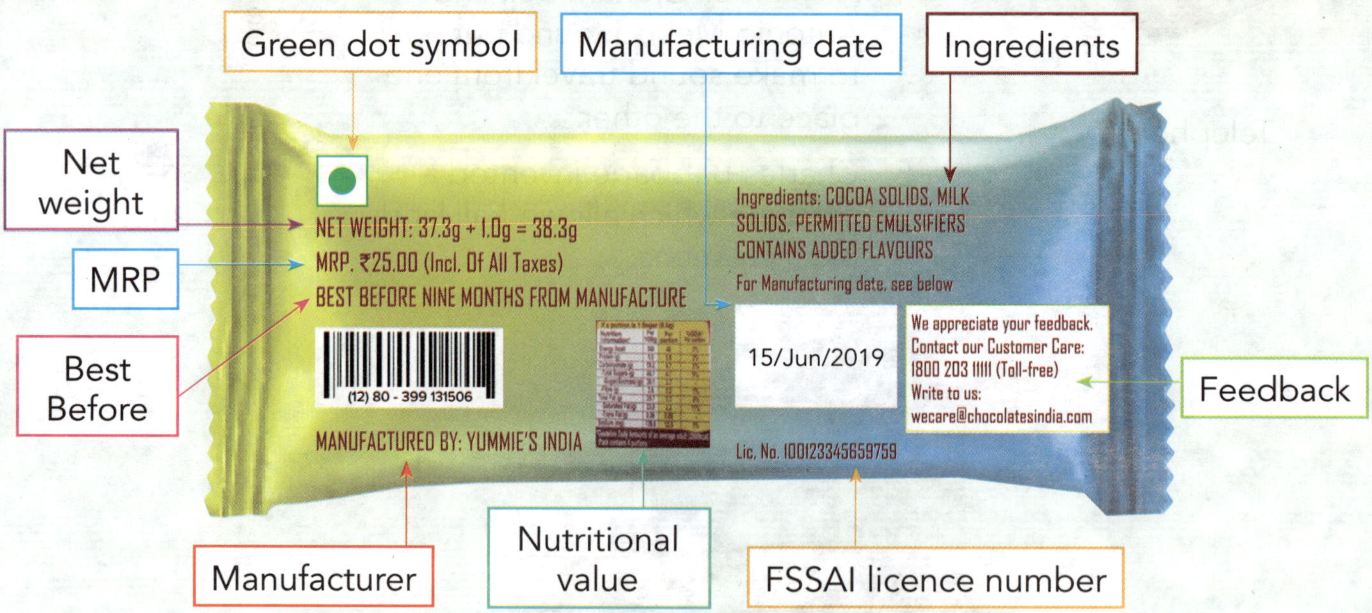

Whiz Fact

The Food Safety and Standards Authority of India (FSSAI) is an organization that decides whether a food product is safe to consume. All packaged food has an FSSAI licence number.

Complete this crossword using the clues about information given on a chocolate wrapper.

Across

1 The food product is fully vegetarian (5, 3)

6 List of food items used to make the product (11)

8 Complaints, suggestions or something nice to say about the product (8)

Down

2 Important nutrients present in the food product (11, 5)

3 Name of the food product and the company that makes it (5, 5)

4 Date before which the product must be eaten (4, 6)

5 Highest price a buyer must pay for the product (3)

7 Total weight of the product in the packet (3, 6)

28 Word Snakes

Word snakes are made by connecting letters of two or more than two words. The last letter of the first word is the first letter of next word. The joining letter is not to be repeated.

Let us make a word snake using the words 'first' and 'thing'.

The word **FIRST**, ends with the letter **T**.

The word **THING**, begins with the letter **T**.

So, FIRSTHING is a word snake.

Let us try to make a longer word snake using four words.

BOOK RUB DOOR LITTLE

- The word **BOOK** begins with **B** and the word **RUB** ends with **B**.
- The word **RUB** begins with **R** and the word **DOOR** ends with **R**.
- As the word **LITTLE** begins with **L** and ends with **E**, which are not the first or last letters of any other word, we cannot use it.

Step 1: Begin by writing any of above given words. Let us choose RUB.

RUB

Step 2: Next, add the word DOOR. Finally, add the word BOOK and the word snake is complete.

DOORUB **DOORUBOOK**

Whiz Fact

The reticulated python is the longest snake in the world.

Make the longest possible word snakes using these words and write them on the snakes. Be careful because not all words can be used.

1 EARTH TAKE NIGHT HAND

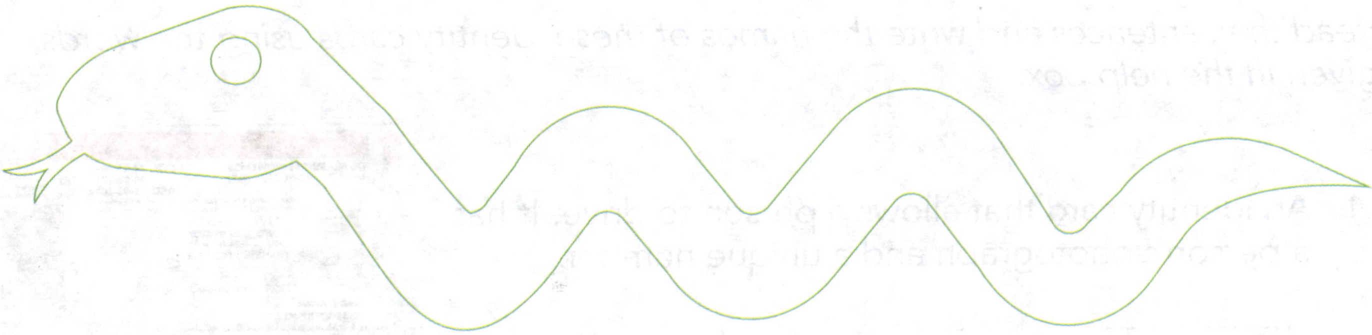

2 KING GATE EAST LOOK

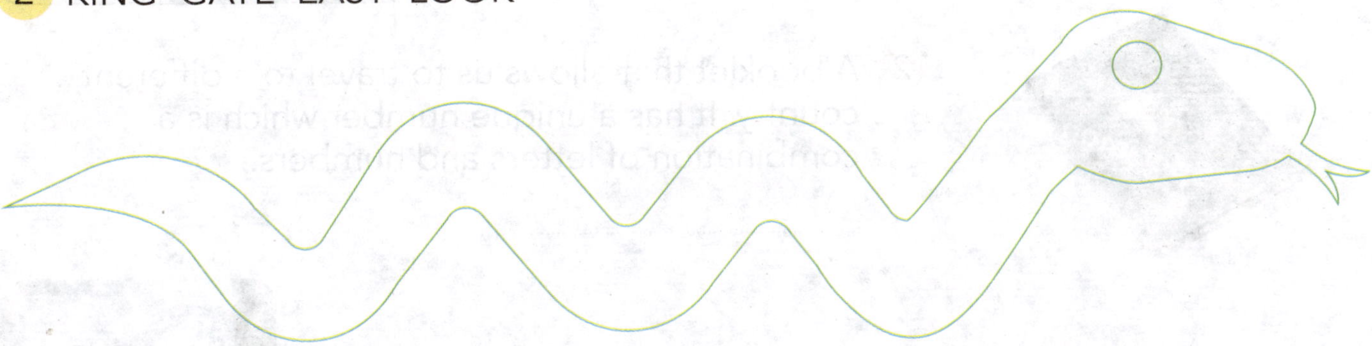

3 RIGHT MELON PAPER BLINK

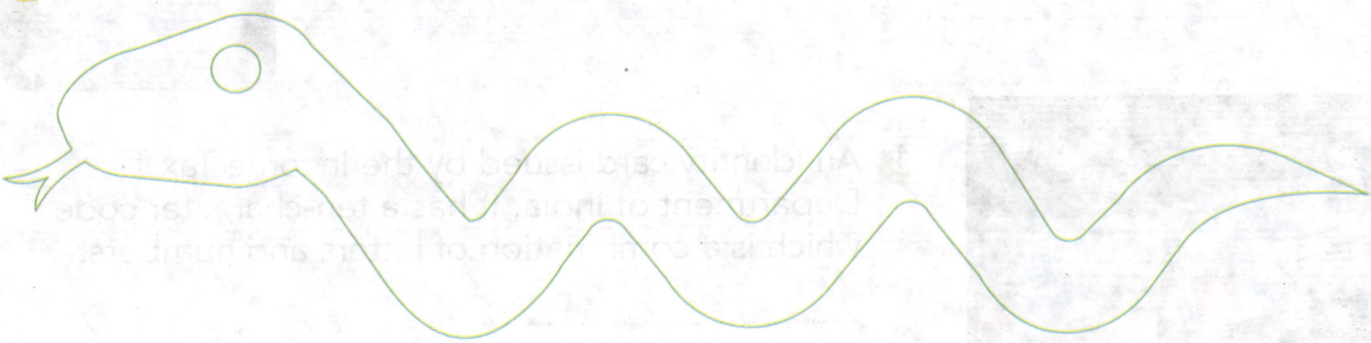

4 BRAIN STORM CLING GRASS

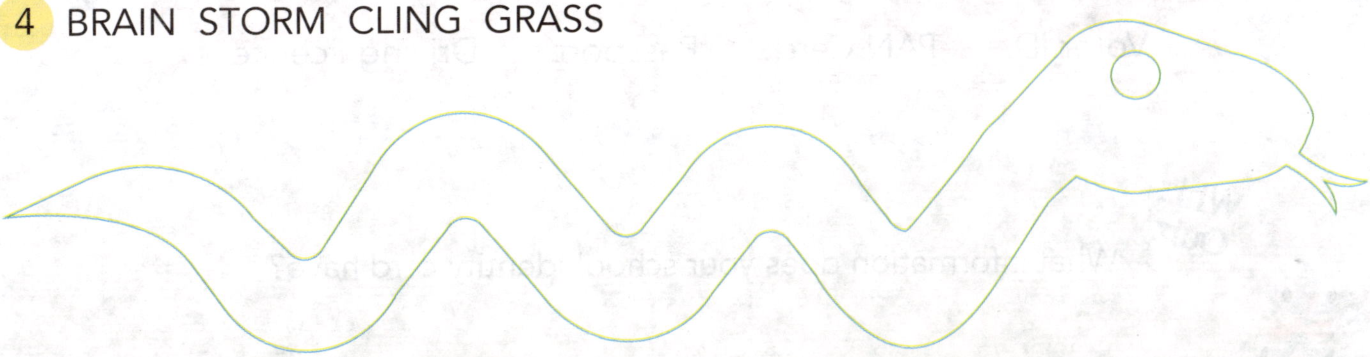

29 Identity Cards

Read the sentences and write the names of these identity cards using the words given in the help box.

1 An identity card that allows a person to drive. It has a person's photograph and a unique number.

....

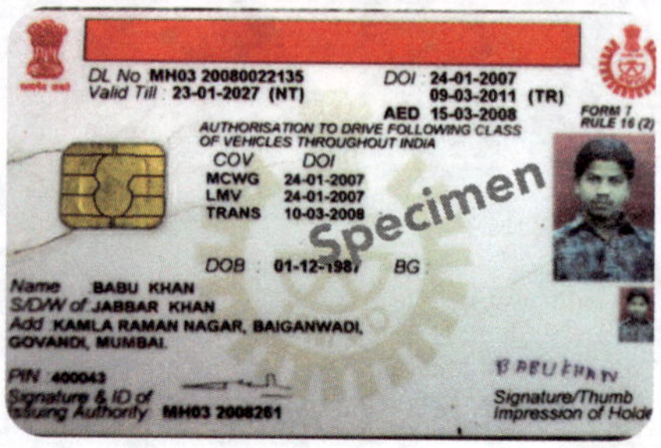

2 A booklet that allows us to travel to a different country. It has a unique number which is a combination of letters and numbers.

....

3 An identity card that allows a person to vote in elections in India.

....

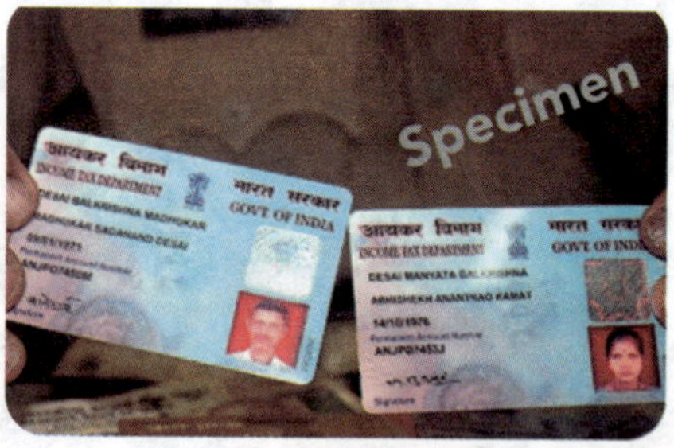

4 An identity card issued by the Income Tax Department of India. It has a ten-character code which is a combination of letters and numbers.

....

Voter ID   PAN Card   Passport   Driving licence

Whiz Quiz

What information does your school identity card have?

30 Countries and Capitals

Here are the six biggest countries in the world with their capitals. Some letters are missing either from the name of the country or the capital. Read the clues and complete the names of these countries and capitals. Each country-capital pair has two blanks that should be filled with the same letters.

1 Russia

The .... gives us milk.

Mos....... ....

2 .... ada

Soft drinks come in a bottle or a ....

Ottawa

3 B....... ....zil

.... is an Egyptian god with a very short name.

B....... ....silia

4 United States of America

If our clothes are dirty, we .... them.

....ington D.C.

5 ....a

Below our lips is our ....

Beijing

6 Australia

A three-letter word which means 'to make a mistake' ....

Canb....... ....a

Whiz Fact

The capital of the island country of Maldives is Malé.

31 Athletic Fun

Athletics are sports that include running, jumping, throwing or walking.

Read the clues and write the names of these athletic sports in the crossword puzzle using the words given in the help box.

Whiz Fact

Steeplechase is an obstacle race that was first played in Ireland. The obstacles used in this foot race include water streams, ditches and fences.

Across

4 A competition in which a long spear is thrown as far as possible

5 A race between two or more teams, each member of the team runs one section of the race

6 A competition in which a metal ball attached to a steel wire is flung as far as possible

7 A long-distance race of over 42 km

8 A leap as far away as possible from a take off point

9 A competition in which a heavy metal ball is pushed into the air as far as possible

Down

1 A competition in which a heavy disc-shaped object is flung as far as possible

2 A race in which runners jump over obstacles

3 An athletics event in which athletes jump over a high bar, using a long flexible pole to help lift themselves up

marathon   javelin throw   hurdles   hammer throw   relay
shot put   discus throw   pole vault   long jump

Whiz Quiz

How many athletic events make a decathlon?

32 Anagrams

An anagram is a word or phrase formed by changing the order of the letters in another word or phrase. For example, 'listen' is an anagram of 'silent'.

Write one anagram using the letters of each of these words. One has been done for you.

1 I N C H

C H I N

2 V A S E

3 A R C

4 B R A G

Now, write two anagrams using the letters of each of these words.

5 O W N

6 O P T

7 F L O W

8 I N K S

9 M E A L

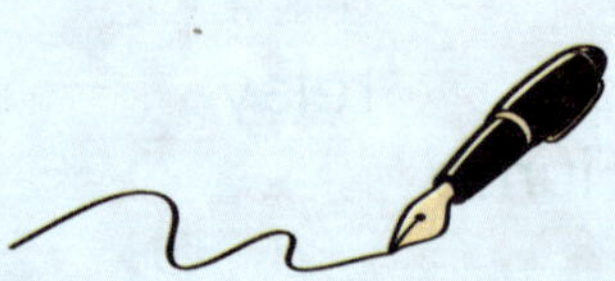

Whiz Fact

A palindrome is a word that is the same whether you read it backwards or forwards, for example the word 'refer'.

33 Delhi

New Delhi is the capital of India. The city of Delhi has many beautiful buildings and monuments.

Match the columns and complete the names of some famous buildings and monuments of Delhi.

1 Qutub ☐

2 Red ☐

3 Lotus ☐

4 India ☐

5 Humayun's ☐

6 Jantar ☐

a Tomb

b Mantar

c Minar

d Temple

e Fort

f Gate

Whiz Quiz Find out the names of the rulers who built these buildings.

34 Closed Lists

Closed lists have a fixed number of things such as days of the week.

Look at these closed lists and fill in the missing words.

1 Months of the Year

- ....
- ....
- ....
- April
- ....
- June
- ....
- ....
- ....
- October
- November
- ....

2 Names of Indian States starting with M

- Meghalaya
- Manipur
- ....
- ....
- ....

3 Chess Pieces

- King
- Rook
- Bishop
- ....
- ....
- ....

4 Primary Colours

- ....
- ....
- ....

5 Suits in a Pack of Cards

- Spades
- Clubs
- ....
- ....

6 Secondary Colours

- ....
- ....
- ....

Whiz Fact

Pluto was once in the list of planets. Scientists decided that it was too small to be a planet. So, the closed list of nine planets is now a closed list of eight planets.

35 Olympics Special

Various sports are played at the Olympics by many countries. Read the lines and match them with the correct pictures.

1 The mascots of the 2021 Olympic Games are superheroes Miraitowa and Someity.

2 The 2016 Olympics were held in Rio de Janeiro.

3 The host of the 2021 Olympics is Tokyo.

4 The Olympics were first held in Athens.

5 The Olympic flag has five rings.

a

b

c

d

e

Whiz Quiz

Write the names of the continents in which these countries are located.

1 Brazil .... 2 Japan ....

3 Greece ....

36 Space and Days

In Hindi, the days of the week are named after some planets, moons and stars.

Read the clues and write the Hindi names of the days of the week. Be careful because the days are jumbled.

1 *Soma* is the Moon	a Sunday ....
2 *Mangal* is Mars	b Friday ....
3 *Budh* is Mercury	c Monday ....
4 *Guru* or *Brihaspati* is Jupiter	d Saturday ....
5 *Shukra* is Venus	e Tuesday ....
6 *Shani* is Saturn	f Wednesday ....
7 *Ravi* is the Sun	g Thursday ....

Whiz Quiz After whom or what are the English days Tuesday, Wednesday, Thursday and Friday named?

37 Going to America

Match these facts about the United States of America. Use the picture clues to find the answers.

1. The Statue of Liberty is in this city ☐

2. The capital of USA is named after this leader ☐

3. The flag of the United States ☐

4. The national anthem of America ☐

5. A place known for its film industry ☐

6. The currency of the USA ☐

7. A state made of islands and volcanoes ☐

a Dollar

b Hawaii

c Hollywood

d Stars and Stripes

e Washington D.C.

f New York

g The Star-Sprangled Banner

Whiz Fact

The National Bird of USA is the bald eagle.

38 Being Safe

Being safe is one of the first things people learn. Babies learn to hold the hand of an adult when they are learning to walk so that they do not fall. There is always more to learn about safety because as we grow, we do more things and go to more places.

Tick (✓) the pictures that show the safer thing to do and write why is it safe.

1

a  ☐

b  ☐

....

2

a  ☐

b  ☐

....

3

a  ☐

b  ☐

....

4

a  ☐

b  ☐

....

5

a  b 

6

a  b 

7

a  b 

8

a  b 

Whiz Fact

While boating, we wear life jackets or safety vests. They are brightly-coloured and we should always wear them for our safety.

39 India Extremes

India is the seventh largest country in the world. *Match the pair of India extremes and write their names using the words given in the help box.*

1. Coldest, Dras, Ladakh, –45°C
2. .... Mount K2, 8,611 m above sea level
3. ...., Mawsynram and Cherrapunji
4. Northernmost point, Siachen Glacier
5. .... point, Ghuar Moti, Gujarat
6. Smallest state, Goa

a. .... point Indira Point, Great Nicobar Island

b. .... Phalodi, Rajasthan, 51°C

c. Lowest, Kuttanad, Kerala, 3 m below sea level

d. ...., state Rajasthan

e. Driest, Thar Desert

f. Easternmost point, Kibithu, Arunachal Pradesh

westernmost | largest | highest | hottest | southernmost | wettest

Whiz Fact

The southernmost point of mainland India is Kanyakumari. The distance between the Siachen Glacier and Kanyakumari is 3,043 km.

40 Green Habits

Read these situations and match them with the environment-friendly actions.

1 You have to gift wrap a book for your friend's birthday	a Grow air-purifying plants around the house
2 You live in a dusty and polluted place	b Organise a carpool or else travel to school together by bus
3 You and your schoolmates from the neighbourhood have to attend a school function on a holiday	c Avoid using plastic or paper cups and plates
4 You need to buy bread and milk from a store	d Use old newspapers and decorate them with colours and ribbons
5 You are travelling by a car on the highway	e Carry a cloth bag while shopping

41 Northeast India

The northeast is one of the most beautiful regions of India. It is connected to the rest of India through a narrow stretch of land in West Bengal. This region has eight states—the Seven Sisters and Sikkim.

Read the clues and fill in the blanks using the words given in the help box.

1 Arunachal Pradesh shares its border with Bhutan, China, and Myanmar. The 400-year-old ....WA.......G Monastery is situated here.

2 Shillong, the capital of Meghalaya, has fresh breezes, hilly roads and misty skies. It is known as the ....OT........ A.......D of the East.

3 The name Mizoram means 'land of the hill people'. Mizoram's state dance is called the cheraw. Dancers jump between long ....MB........O sticks.

4 Nagaland shares a boundary with Assam, Arunachal Pradesh and Myanmar. The ................RNB.......L....... Festival is celebrated in this state.

5 Manipur shares a border with Myanmar. The royal game of ……………LO played on horseback originated in this state.

6 The Kaziranga National Park, the home of the one-horned ………HI………O is in Assam.

7 In the tiny state of Tripura, most of the people speak either Kokborok or ………EN………AL……… .

8 Sikkim lies in the lap of the majestic Himalayas. The third-highest mountain peak in the world, the ………AN CH………NJ………NG……… looms over this state.

Hornbill	Kanchenjunga	Tawang	Scotland
Bengali	rhino	polo	bamboo

Whiz Fact

The river Brahmaputra flows through two northeastern states of India—Assam and Arunachal Pradesh.

42 Mind and Body

Write the names of these exercise poses using the words given in the help box.

1 ....

2 ....

3 ....

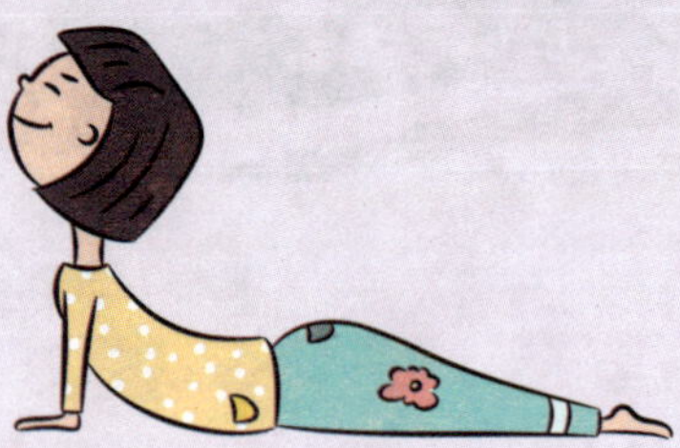

4 ....

5 ....

6 ....

plank tree pose bow pose cobra pose warrior pose cow pose

Whiz Fact

When we hold an exercise pose for long, our muscles become tired and start trembling. Practising exercise everyday can make our muscles stronger.

43 Sri Lanka, Here I Come!

Sri Lanka is India's neighbouring country to its south. Look at the map of Sri Lanka and fill in the blanks with the correct answers.

1. The flag of Sri Lanka has a .... lion/tiger.
2. The capital of Sri Lanka is .... Colombo/ Sigiriya.
3. Sri Lanka has a .... cold/warm climate.
4. Sri Lanka .... is/is not an island country.
5. The .... Palk Strait/ Bering Strait separates India from Sri Lanka.
6. Sri Lanka produces large quantities of .... coffee/tea.
7. .... Ceylon/Bali is the old name of Sri Lanka.
8. .... Blue lotus/ Marigold is the national flower of Sri Lanka.

Whiz Fact

The Sri Lankan flag is symbolic of the native people of Sri Lanka, the Sinhalese.

४४ Rabindranath Tagore

Here are some lines on the life of Rabindranath Tagore. Put them in the correct order to learn about this great Indian.

Rabindranath Tagore

Visva-Bharati University

1 He won the Nobel Prize in Literature in 1913 for his beautiful collection of poems called *Gitanjali*. [ ]

2 He founded the Visva-Bharati University at Santiniketan in 1921. [ ]

3 A song written by Tagore called *Jana Gana Mana* was sung in public in 1911. It later became the national anthem of India. [ ]

4 He died on 7 August, 1941 in Kolkata. [ ]

5 Rabindranath Tagore was born on 7 May, 1861 in Kolkata. [ ]

Whiz Fact

Rabindranath Tagore preferred to learn without schooling, punishment and classes. He is also known as *Gurudev*, which means 'teacher'.

45 Oceans of the World

Five oceans cover more than 70 per cent of the Earth's surface.

Look at the map of the oceans of the world and fill in the blanks.

1. The .... is the largest ocean in the world. It has more than half of all the ocean waters in the world.
2. The .... is the smallest and the shallowest ocean in the world.
3. The ocean that surrounds Antarctica is called the .... Ocean. It got its name in the year 2000.
4. The .... Ocean was the first ocean that was circumnavigated by a ship and an aeroplane.
5. The .... Ocean is bounded by Africa on the west, Asia on the north and Australia on the east. It is the warmest ocean in the world.

Whiz Fact

The Southern Ocean is also called the Antarctic Ocean or the Austral Ocean. Antarctic means the opposite of Arctic and Austral means south.

46 Sudoku

Sudoku is a Japanese number puzzle. It has three columns and three rows in which numbers from 1 to 9 are arranged randomly without being repeated.

In this Sudoku puzzle, a square is empty. Therefore, we must look for the missing number, which is 7.

1	5	8
4	2	9
	3	6

Find the missing numbers to solve these Sudoko puzzles.

1

7	6	3
4		5
8	2	6

2

9	5	7
2	8	
1	3	6

3

2	6	
4	5	1
7	3	8

Whiz Fact

The first ever printed Sudoku puzzle appeared in a London-based newspaper called *The Times*.

Quiz Yourself 1

Fill in the blanks with the correct answers.

1 .... is a northeastern state that shares its border with Bhutan, China, and Myanmar.

2 .... has five arms and looks like a star.

3 A .... is an identity card that allows a person to drive.

4 An .... is a sea creature with eight limbs.

5 .... is also known as an 'ice giant'.

6 .... is a children's horror fiction series by R. L. Stine.

7 The new ₹2000 banknote has a .... colour.

8 .... is the capital of Australia.

9 Rabindranath Tagore won the Nobel Prize in Literature in ....

10 A bear is an ....

11 Koneru Humpy plays ....

12 The Taj Mahal is located on the river ....

13 The sound that hyenas make is called a ....

14 .... is a bear from Darkest Peru.

15 .... was known as the Nightingale of India.

Quiz Yourself 2

Fill in the blanks with the correct answers.

1. P. V. Sindhu is a .... player.
2. The .... separates India from Sri Lanka.
3. .... is a movie about Dracula, lots of monsters and one human.
4. .... was the first Prime Minister of India.
5. .... is a famous children's book with horse as its the main character.
6. The Taj Mahal was built using the white marble from ....
7. .... is known as the Missile Man of India.
8. .... is the easternmost point of India.
9. .... is the capital of Meghalaya.
10. .... is the longest river in India.
11. .... is the capital of Canada.
12. .... is a ball game played with a stick that has a net attached to it.
13. Sri Lanka produces large quantities of ....
14. .... learnt dance from Anna Pavlova.
15. .... is the national anthem of the USA.

Answer Key

Page 9: 1. two; 2. too; 3. there; 4. their; 5. it's; 6. its

Page 10-11: 1. jackfruit; 2. papaya; 3. cherry; 4. mango; 5. strawberry; 6. guava; 7. apricot; 8. pumpkin; 9. spinach; 10. cabbage; 11. capsicum; 12. cauliflower; 13. potato

Page 12-13: Answers will vary

Page 14-15: 1. chatter; 2. click; 3. trumpet; 4. crow; 5. honk; 6. bark; 7. laugh; 8. sing; 9. squeak; 10. croak

Page 16-17: 1. bones; 2. heart; 3. brain; 4. skin; 5. spine; 6. stomach; 7. lungs

Page 18: 1. H; 2. O; 3. C; 4. O; 5. H; 6. H; 7. O; 8. C; 9. C; 10. O; 11. C

Page 19: 1. Monopoly; 2. Lego; 3. Scrabble; 4. Ludo; 5. Jenga; 6. Battleship; 7. Carrom; 8. Chess; 9. Snakes and Ladders

Page 20-21: 1. frangipani; 2. drumstick flower; 3. gulmohar flower; 4. daffodil; 5. pansy; 6. clove flower; 7. bougainvillea; 8. hibiscus

Page 22-23: 1. *The Jungle Book*; 2. *Alice's Adventures in Wonderland*; 3. *Gulliver's Travels*; 4. *Stuart Little*; 5. *Winnie-the-Pooh*; 6. *Charlotte's Web*; 7. *Peter Pan*; 8. *Pippi Longstockings*; 9. *A Bear Called Paddington*; 10. *Black Beauty*

Page 24-25: 1. President, scientist; 2. Kolkata, Nobel Peace Prize; 3. Kalakshetra, ballet; 4. hockey, gold; 5. Nightingale, poet; 6. Prime Minister, Children's Day

Page 26-27: 1. octopus; 2. whale; 3. starfish; 4. jellyfish; 5. seahorse; 6. shark; 7. oyster; 8. crab

Page 28-29: 1. polo; 2. rugby; 3. bowling; 4. squash; 5. billiards; 6. basketball; 7. hockey; 8. golf; 9. tennis; 10. volleyball

Page 30-31: 1. 0, 2; 2. 1, 55; 3. 2, 10; 4. 3, 10; 5. 4, 25; 6. 1, 20; 7. 1, 25

Page 32: 1. *Goosebumps*; 2. *Casper*; 3. *Hotel Transylvania*; 4. *The Witches*; 5. *Maleficent*

Page 33: 2, 3, 5, 6, 7, 8, 10, 11, 14, 16, 18, 19

Page 34: 1. mausoleum; 2. Yamuna; 3. marble; 4. dome; 5. minarets; 6. gardens

Page 35: 1. save file; 2. cut; 3. copy; 4. paste; 5. undo; 6. redo; 7. print; 8. close file

Page 36-37: 1. penguin, it cannot fly; 2. shark, it does not live on land; 3. monkey, it has hair on its body; 4. dolphin, it breathes with lungs; 5. spider, it has eight legs; 6. jellyfish, its body is not covered with a shell

Page 38-39: 1. tennis; 2. wrestling; 3. badminton; 4. cricket; 5. shooting; 6. chess; 7. golf; 8. boxing

Page 40-41: 1. ; 2. ; 3. ; 4. ; 5. 

Page 42-43: 2. raincoat; 3. armchair; 4. inkpot; 5. wheelbarrow; 6. necklace; 7. buckle; 8. wallet; 9. sandwich; 10. toast

Page 44: 1. north; 2. east; 3. west; 4. centre; 5. south

Page 45: 2. d, Hampi with Chariot; 3. b, Sanchi Stupa;

4. a, Magalyaan; 5. e, Rani Ki Vav; 6. f, Red Fort

Page 46-47: 1. ouch!; 2. ta-da!; 3. eek!; 4. boo-hoo!; 5. yahoo!; 6. oh no!; 7. wow!; 8. shh!

Page 48-49: 1. Mercury; 2. Venus; 3. Earth; 4. Mars; 5. Jupiter; 6. Saturn; 7. Uranus; 8. Neptune

Page 50-51: 1. b; 2. a; 3. e; 4. c; 5. c; 6. d

Page 52-53: Across: 1. green dot; 6. ingredients; 8. feedback

Down: 2. nutritional value; 3. brand name; 4. best before; 5. MRP; 7. net weight

Page 54-55: 1. NIGHTAKEARTHAND; 2. LOOKINGATEAST; 3. PAPERIGHT; 4. CLINGRASSTORM

Page 56: 1. driving licence; 2. passport; 3. Voter ID; 4. Pan Card

Page 57: 1. cow, Moscow; 2. Canada, can; 3. Brazil, Ra; Brasilia; 4. wash, Washington D.C.; 5. China, chin; 6. err, Canberra

Page 58-59: Across: 4. javelin throw; 5. relay; 6. hammer throw; 7. marathon; 8. long jump; 9. shot put

Down: 1. discus throw; 2. hurdles; 3. pole vault

Page 60: 2. save; 3. car; 4. grab; 5. now, won; 6. top, pot; 7. wolf; fowl; 8. sink, skin; 9. male, lame

Page 61: 1. c; 2. e; 3. d; 4. f; 5. a; 6. b

Page 62: 1. January, February, March, May, July, August, September, December; 2. Maharashtra, Madhya Pradesh, Mizoram; 3. Pawns, King, Knight; 4. purple, orange, green; 5. diamonds, stars; 6. red, yellow, blue

Page 63: 1. b; 2. e; 3. a; 4. c; 5. d

Page 64: 1. Somvar; 2. Mangalwaar; 3. Budhwaar; 4. Guruwaar; 5. Shukravaar; 6. Shanivar; 7. Ravivar

Page 65: 1. f; 2. e; 3. g; 4. c; 5. c; 6. a; 7. b

Page 66-67: 1. b, walking on footpath; 2. a, not keeping hands out of a vehicle; 3. b, crossing road at a zebra crossing; 4. a, wearing a helmet while riding scooter; 5. b, wearing a seatbelt; 6. b, walking in the same direction as others; 7. a, not listening to loud music on a bus; 8. b, cleaning hands before eating food

Page 68: 1. b, hottest; 2. c, highest; 3. e, wettest; 4. a, southernmost; 5. f, westernmost; 6. d, largest

Page 69: 1. d; 2. a; 3. b; 4. c; 5. c

Page 70-71: 1. Tawang; 2. Scotland; 3. bamboo; 4. Hornbill; 5. Polo; 6. rhino; 7. Bengali; 8. Kanchenjunga

Page 72: 1. tree pose; 2. warrior pose; 3. plank pose; 4. cobra pose; 5. cow pose; 6. bow pose

Page 73: 1. lion; 2. Colombo; 3. warm; 4. is; 5. Palk Strait; 6. tea; 7. Ceylon; 8. Blue Lotus

Page 74: 1. c; 2. d; 3. b; 4. e; 5. a

Page 75: 1. Pacific Ocean; 2. Arctic Ocean; 3. Southern Ocean; 4. Atlantic; 5. Indian

Page 76: 1. 1; 2. 4; 3. 9

Page 77: 1. Arunachal Pradesh; 2. starfish; 3. driving licence; 4. octopus; 5. Uranus; 6. *Goosebumps*; 7. magenta; 8. Canberra; 9. 1913; 10. omnivore; 11. chess; 12. Yamuna; 13. laugh; 14. Paddington; 15. Sarojini Naidu

Page 78: 1. badminton; 2. Palk Strait; 3. *Hotel Transylvania*; 4. Jawaharlal Nehru; 5. *Black Beauty*; 6. Makrana; 7. A.P.J. Abdul Kalam; 8. Kibithu; 9. Shillong; 10. Brahmaputra; 11. Ottawa; 12. Lacrosse; 13. coffee; 14. Rukmini Devi Arundale; 15. The Star-Sprangled Banner